T0086997

THE OXFORD PIANO METHOD

P·I·A·N·O T·I·M·E
S·I·G·H·T-R·E·A·D·I·N·G

B·O·O·K 3

Pauline Hall and Fiona Macardle

Music Department
OXFORD UNIVERSITY PRESS
Great Clarendon Street, Oxford OX2 6DP

Oxford University Press, Great Clarendon Street, Oxford OX2 6DP, England
Oxford University Press Inc., 198 Madison Avenue, New York, NY 10016, USA

Oxford is a trade mark of Oxford University Press

© Oxford University Press 1996

All rights reserved. Apart from any fair dealing for the purposes of research or private study, or criticism or review, as permitted under the Copyright, Designs and Patents Act, 1988, this publication may only be reproduced, stored, or transmitted, in any form or by any means, with the prior permission in writing of Oxford University Press.

Permission to perform the work in public (except in the course of divine worship) should normally be obtained from the Performing Right Society Ltd. (PRS), 29/33 Berners Street, London W1P 4AA, or its affiliated Societies in each country throughout the world, unless the owner or the occupier of the premises being used holds a licence from the Society.

Permission to make a recording must be obtained in advance from the Mechanical Copyright Protection Society Ltd. (MCPS), Elgar House, 41 Streatham High Road, London SW16 1ER, or its affiliated Societies in each country throughout the world.

ISBN 978-0-19-372770-0

24

Music originated by Seton Music Graphics Ltd., Ireland

Book design by Barbara Prentiss

Printed in Great Britain on acid-free paper by
Halstan & Co. Ltd., Amersham, Bucks

INTRODUCTION

Congratulations! You have safely pioneered your way through the hazards of Books 1 and 2, and now Book 3 lies ahead!

Your challenge in this book is to be able to do without the printed code-signs used in Books 1 and 2, but to do all your checking as if they were still there to remind you.

Here is a map with a message. Say it regularly to yourself and it will guide you through any panic stages.

And your **TWO GOLDEN RULES:**

1. Count steadily as you play
2. Never stop or look back!

Remember the secret code-signs we used in Books 1 and 2? Here is a list of them to remind you. Get used to checking **everything** before you set off on each piece.

What key—sharps or flats?

Time—keep it steady

Ties—any tied notes?

Rhythm—there may be tricky rhythms ahead

Rests—look out for them

Fingering—look ahead and be ready

Skips or jumps—look out!

Leger lines

Expression—makes music sound **'musical'**

Accidentals—don't be caught out

Lk out!

These code-signs will be at the beginning of each stage, so you may sometimes have to look back to remind yourself. Some of the pieces will have their own code-sign beside them as an extra reminder.

STAGE 1

Measuring up

Have you ever looked at different maps and noticed that although the maps may be of the same area, the scale may be different? One may be large covering a whole page, whilst another may be small enough to fit into your pocket. Music can be a bit like this.

We're going to have a go at sight-reading in $\frac{3}{8}$ time. It's the same as $\frac{3}{4}$ except that instead of counting in crotchets, we count in **quavers**.

Play this:

You will find that it sounds exactly the same as this:

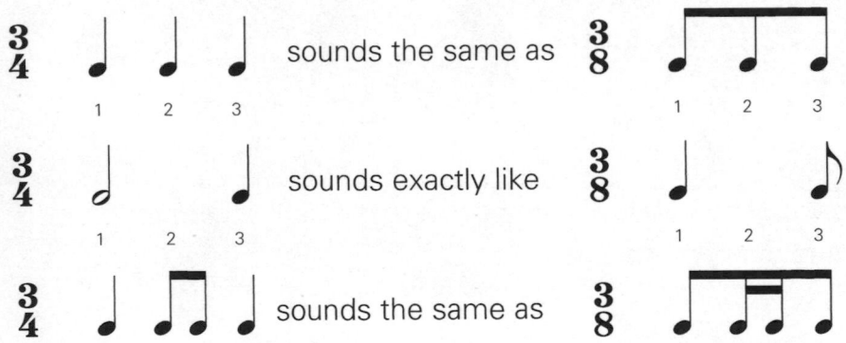

Get it?

Which of these pairs of tunes sound exactly the same? **LOOK** OUT!—there might be a catch!

1
mf
p
2
3 LOOK OUT! This is a new key—D—with two sharps.
4
5

Remember that in $\frac{3}{8}$, 𝄾 is **1 count.**

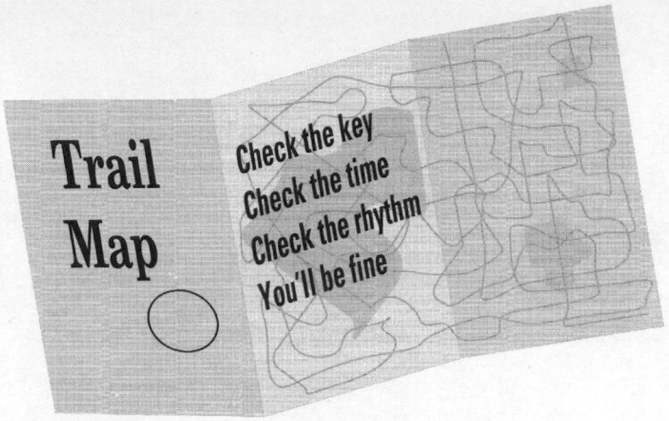

6 Count out two bars before you start to play.

7

8 👓 Rests.

9

You should now be very familiar with this rhythm: 

Here's the same rhythm in 

Sometimes you'll find this rhythm:  Can you work it out?

(It's very easy to get  and  muddled up. Always look out for the dotted note which will be the longest one.)

Here are two sound-alikes:

Now it's left hand's chance to venture out alone!

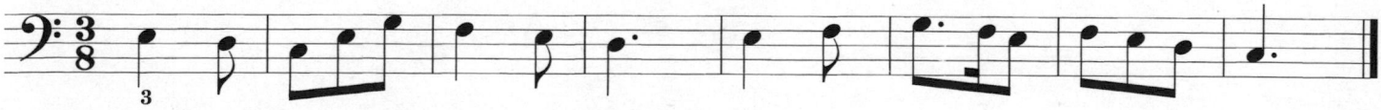

G·U·E·S·S A·N·D P·L·A·Y

☞ *for two players* ☜

Scattered round the page are lots of short bits of music. They're all different. The aim of the game is to see if you can listen first and then spot the one that's just been played.

You need two players:	Player A	Shut your eyes and **listen hard**!
	Player B	Play one of the tunes (twice).
	Player A	Open your eyes and look carefully. Which one was played? Guess! Were you right? If so, well done!

Now change places.

STAGE 2

Questions and answers

In this stage both hands have quite a lot to do, so plenty of careful looking and checking BEFORE you place your hands.

Some of these pieces are in 'question–and–answer' form, whilst some are 'chasers'. Look carefully. Try to bring out the tune even if it is in the left hand. Pretend you are playing these for an exam. An examiner might have heard these pieces played very badly at least twenty times already today. Give them a treat—make these pieces a pleasure to listen to!

1

2 ♭s in both hands.

3

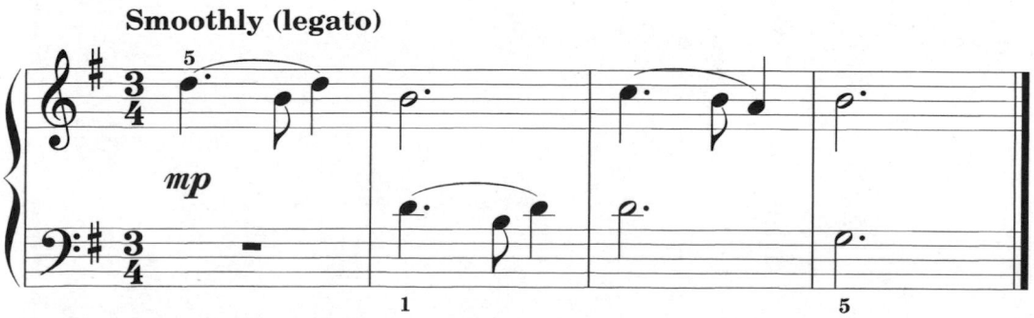

Because you've collected so many code-signs, we're dropping three of them  but keep checking before you play, as if they were still there.

7 The last note in a piece very often gets cut short! Make sure you hold it on for its full value.

8

9 Check how many counts the rests are worth before you begin! Which hand plays a black note?

10

11

A M·U·S·I·C·A·L W·O·R·D P·U·Z·Z·L·E

Have a little break and try out your word skills. There is a clue for each word which goes across. When you have completed these words you will find the name of something you know well, written in the middle column.

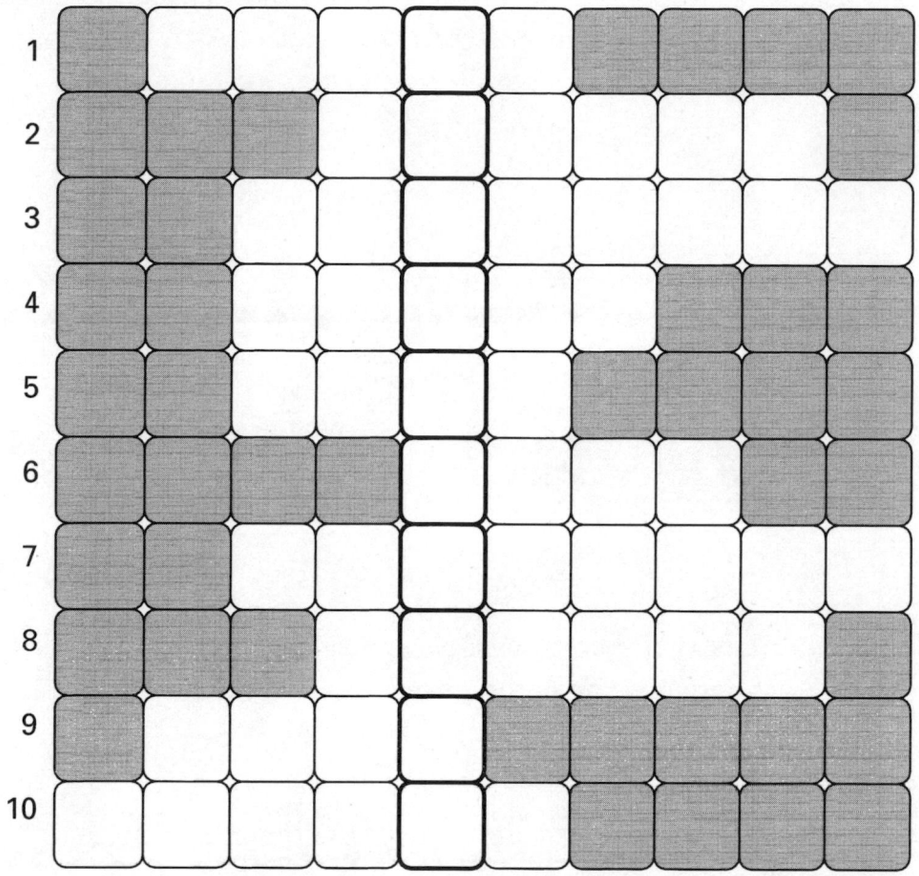

Clues

1 The Italian word for 'time'.

2 A stringed instrument.

3 How would you play this note? 𝅗𝅥.

4 Slow.

5 A wind instrument.

6 ♭

7 𝅗𝅥

8 𝄞 This is a _____ clef.

9 𝄽

10 𝅘𝅥𝅮

Answers: Tempo; Violin; Staccato; Lento; Oboe; Flat; Crotchet; Treble; Rest; Quaver.

Show time

By now you are more used to rests. This stage has six very short but pleasant pieces which you might like to play to someone else.

Get used to someone else listening to your playing—it can be quite nerve-racking, so plan each piece carefully and check everything in advance. Better still, also try to hear the piece in your head before playing it to your audience.

1

2 Don't confuse a **phrase-mark** with a tie. They look very similar, but a phrase-mark is over a group of **different notes,** and a tie is between **the same notes**—holding them on.

3

No more code-signs from now on but don't stop looking out for expression marks.
After all does mean something, and there is a great difference between ***p*** and ***f***!

4 In a piece where there are lots of rests you must count out loud (even if it's only a whisper).

Like a dance

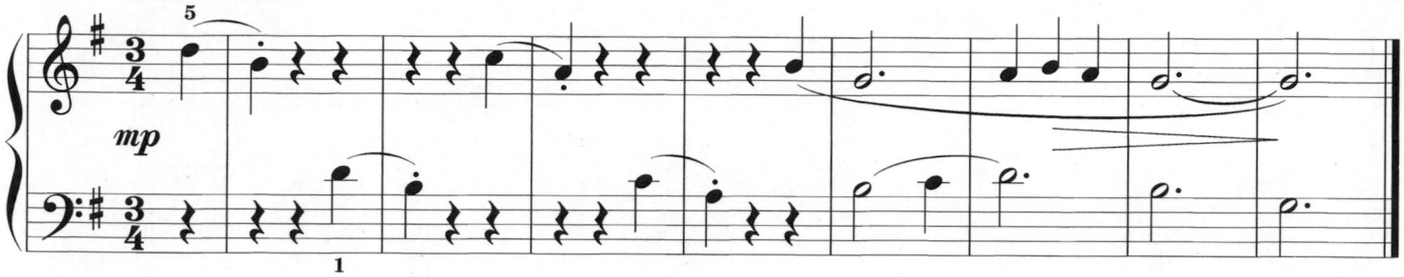

5 Double-check that you can do the right-hand rhythm in the second-to-last bar.

Andante

6 Any black keys? Which hand? Count out bar 4 carefully before you start.

Beware! Both hands off!

7 Imagine you're a teacher! Your pupil needs lots of help with sight-reading but the code-signs have somehow got left out in the next piece!

Draw the four signs that you think would be the most helpful:

STAGE 4

Striding out

To some people, intervals bigger than a second can look the same. Look carefully at the examples below and compare them.

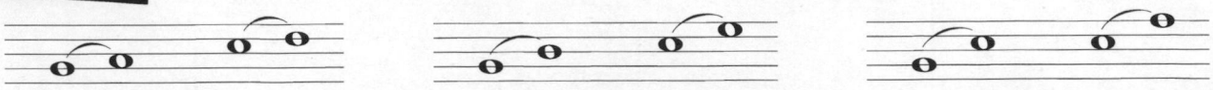

seconds thirds fourths

Test your observation

Go through the bars below and say, as quickly as you can, whether you think they are seconds, thirds, or fourths. Then go back and write the intervals below, checking as you go. Last of all, play them.

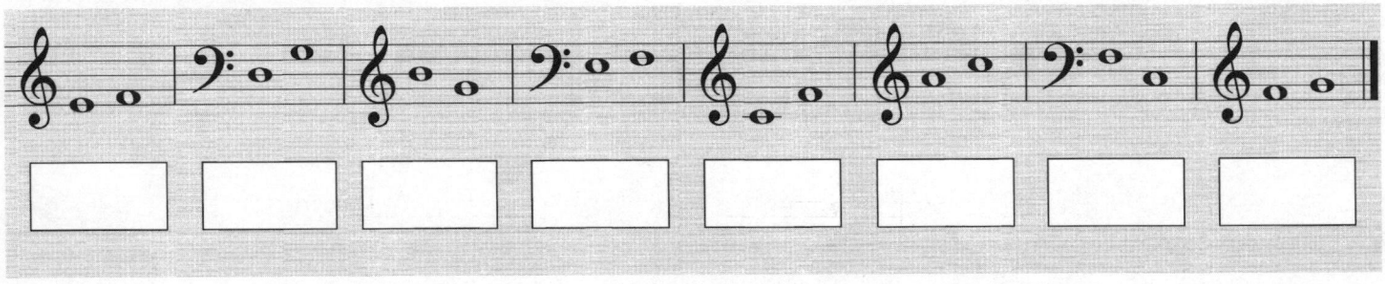

Check where the fourths are in the next piece before you begin.

1 Any black keys?

2

When in doubt—count it out!

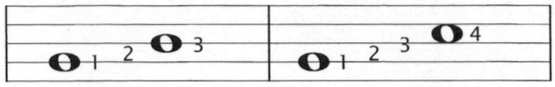

a third a fourth

3

In march time

mf

4

Lively

mf

5

Grazioso

mp *mf*

6

Legato

rall.

mp

Are you remembering to check the key and time signatures of **every** piece before you do anything else?

STAGE 5

Easy does it

Some of these are just a little more difficult.
Don't panic—prepare well!
Make sure you don't advance too fast into unknown territory!

1 Lots of B♭s.

Con moto

The next pieces are all in $\frac{6}{8}$ time—the first time you have come across this time signature.

It isn't difficult if you remember a few things:

- Each bar $\frac{6}{8}$ is only the same as two $\frac{3}{8}$ bars stuck together.
- Until you are happy with $\frac{6}{8}$ time count six quavers in a bar. 1 2 3 4 5 6
- Remember ♩. = ♫
- Be careful—a crotchet ♩ is worth ♫ so you should look out for ♩ ♪ ♩ ♪ 1 2 3 4 5 6

2

3 F♯s.

Perhaps you know the next tune. LOOK out for the accidental in the last bar.

Can you convert the next $\frac{6}{8}$ tune into $\frac{3}{8}$ by adding some new barlines and changing the time signature? Play it first.

Play it again after it becomes $\frac{3}{8}$. Does it sound any different?

7 Don't forget a **quaver** rest 𝄾 (it looks a bit like a funny figure 7).

STAGE 6

Jumping for joy!

Once you can manage a FIFTH, other intervals seem easy!

You have already been using fifths in the bass—but from now on we use them and larger intervals for both hands. A fifth is just two thirds stuck together!

When in doubt—count it out!

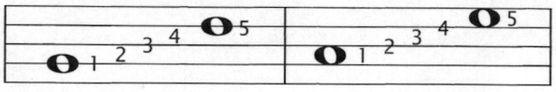

a 'line' fifth a 'space' fifth

Here's a diagram to help you

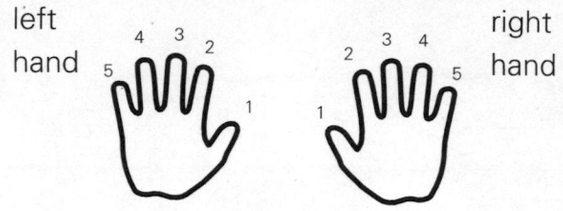

Quick as you can—what are these intervals?
(Name them first, and then write the answers in the boxes underneath.)

From now on we're leaving out the rest sign  but this doesn't mean there are no more rests!

1 Don't let left hand get caught out.

2

3

4 How many times does the left hand play F♯?

A quick look at LEGER LINES

These scare some people—but there's no need to be nervous of them.
Just get used to one or two important ones:

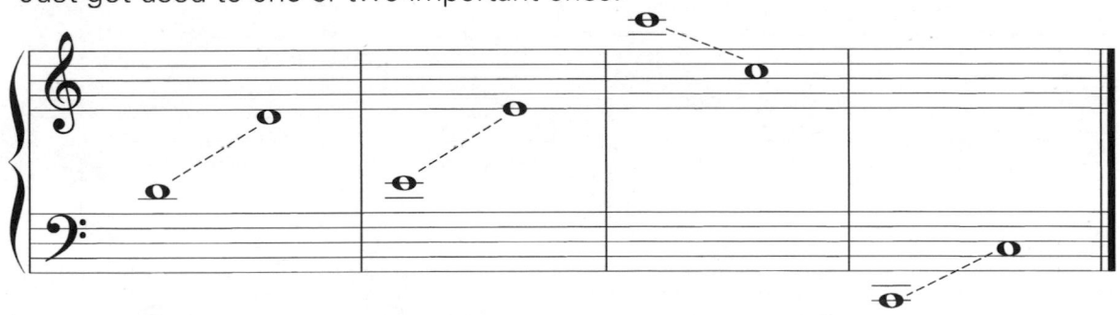

Same note Same note An octave above An octave below

Quick as you can! Find and play these:

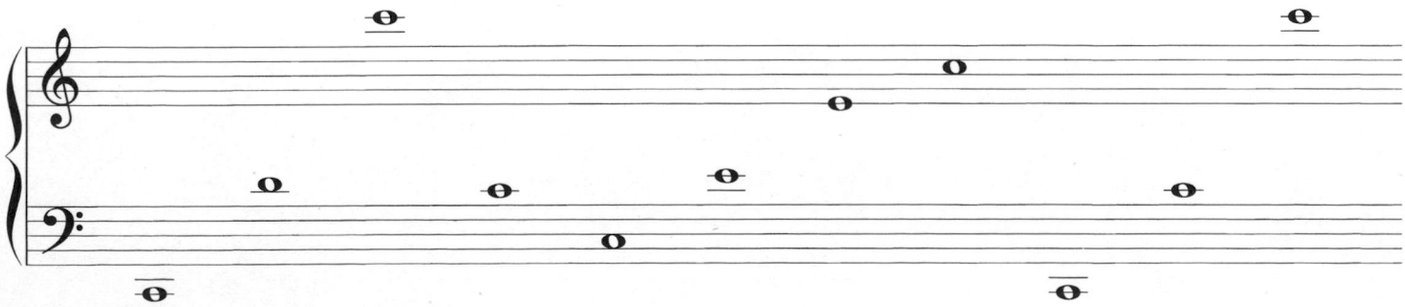

Can you train yourself to look ahead and remember?
It's a great help when you're sight-reading.

In the boxes below are some short music patterns. The game is to look at one for two seconds. Shut your eyes. Play it! Get your hand ready before you begin. Ready?

Now they're getting a bit harder!

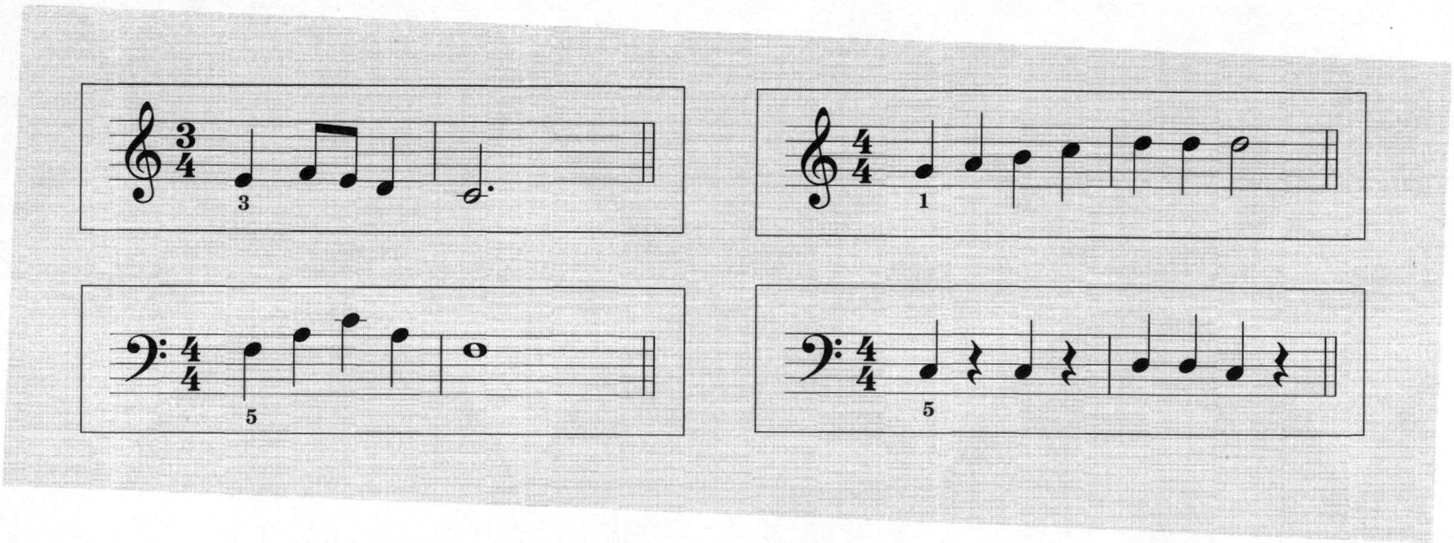

And a really difficult one! Give yourself five seconds to look (spot the way the notes are in a pattern):

You can try this memory game with any music.

STAGE 7

Reaching out

At this stage, changing the position of your hands is probably the most frightening thing! Having been used to being in one place for the whole piece, your hand must move—sometimes once, sometimes more often. These moves are usually marked with fresh fingering. NOTE THEM WELL. Move your hand silently from one place to the other, once you have decided which hand is moving where!

Remember this code-sign?

Remember! If you find any of these pieces just too difficult, pencil in a reminder in the margin and ask your teacher to help you.

1

Largo

mp

New hand position. Left hand moves down one note then stays.

2

Moderato

p *mf*

3

Andante

rit.

One of the sneakiest ways to move the position of your hand is by the interval of a **sixth**. Your whole hand moves up one note which can be very off-putting if you forget that you've got yourself one step further up the keyboard!

A sixth looks like this:

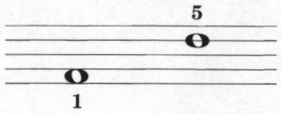

and there are four notes between your thumb and fifth finger.

Can you spot the sixths amongst this lot?

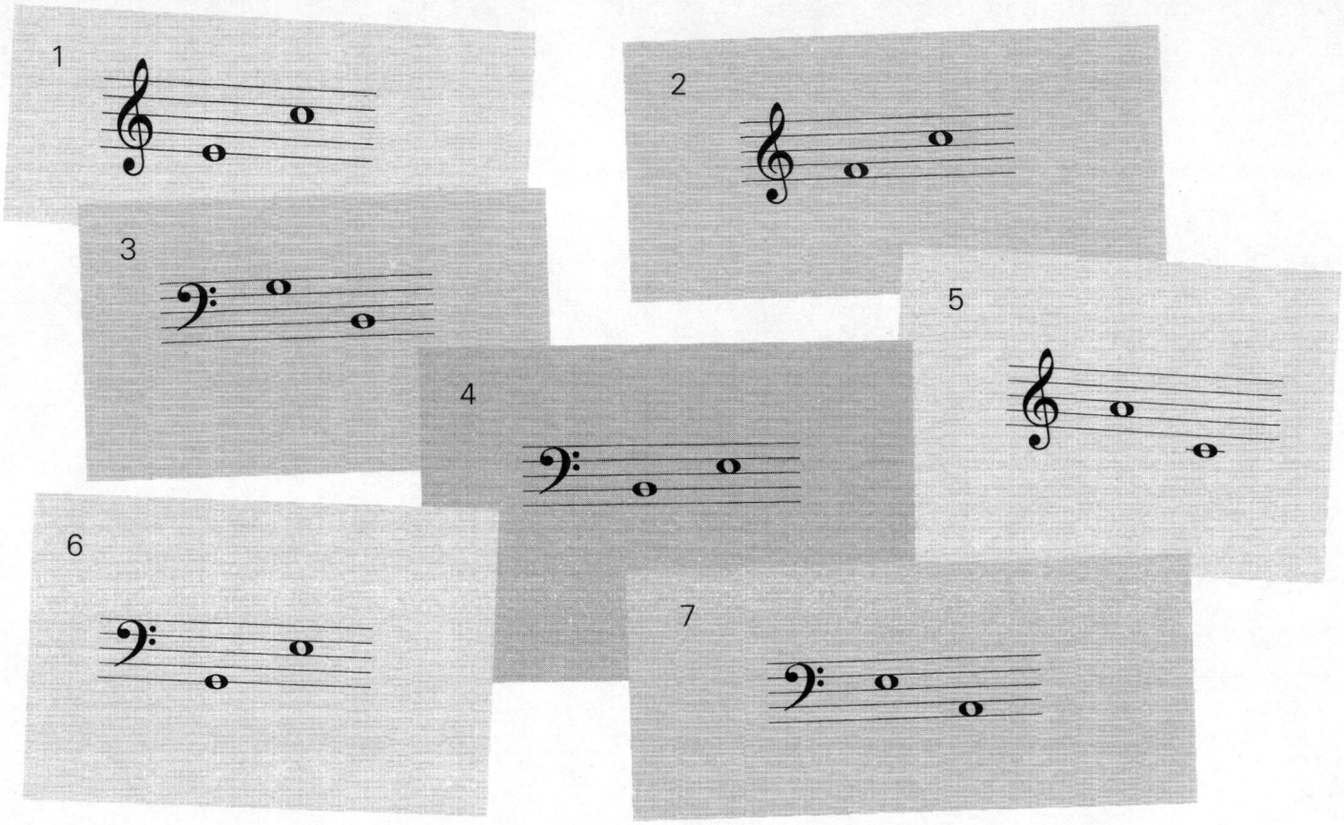

Do you recognize this tune?

4

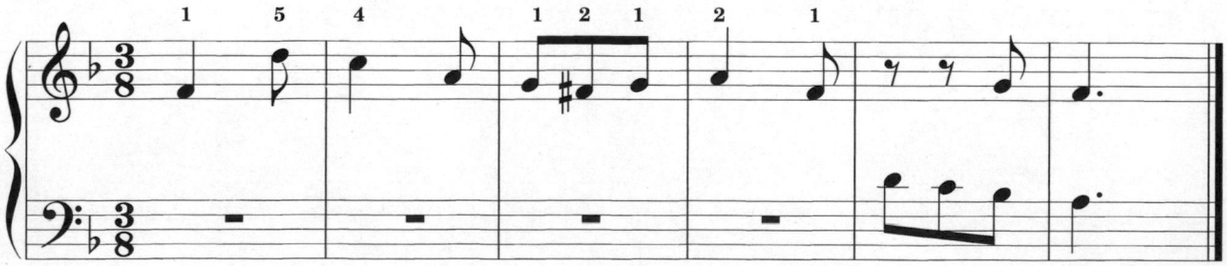

5 In the last two bars the left hand has some big stretches.

6

7

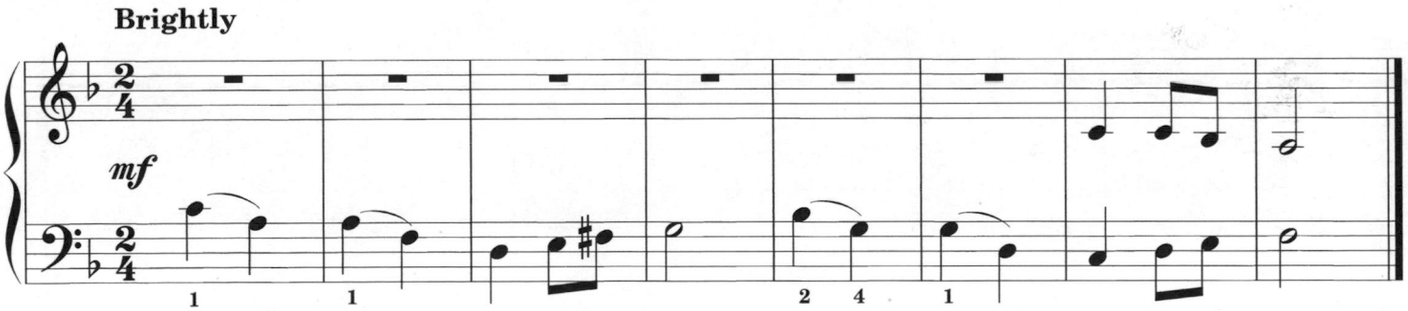

WELL DONE! That stage wasn't easy, but the trick is now to go back and try to sight-read the pieces in the early books that you didn't learn, and any other easy-ish music you can lay your hands on.

There are so many pieces in this book you could even go back and play them again. Then you will see just how far you have come to reach this stage! NOW PLOUGH ON!!

Approaching the summit

We're going to drop the code-sign for the little jumping man from now on. Look out for jumps just the same—there are plenty of thirds, fourths, fifths and even sixths about!

AAARGH!! IT'S MOVED!!

This is the feeling you sometimes gets when sight-reading. You're going along doing well—or so you think—and then one of the hands moves miles away and you panic —"Aaargh! Where am I now?" Then you must re-adjust your mind and carry on. Think how much **easier** it would be if you looked through the piece (especially if it's a short one) and **checked these things before you started!**

1

2

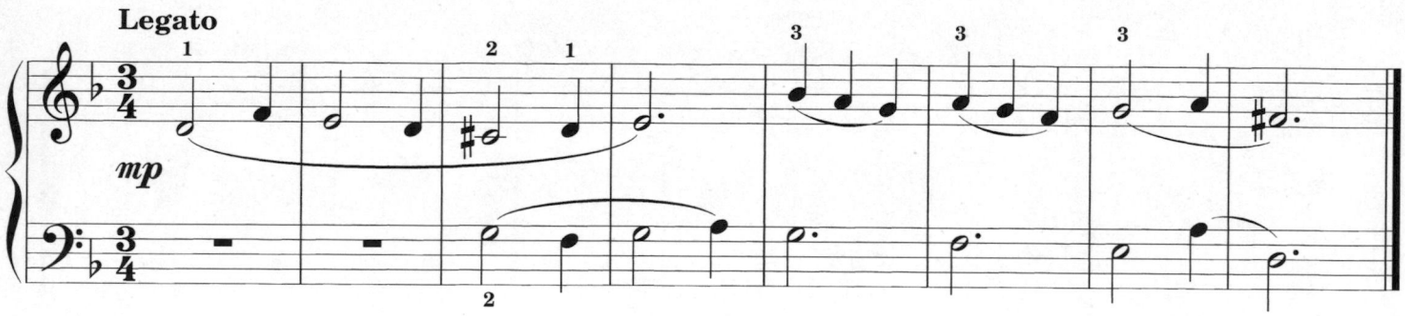

3

If you don't know the notes here, look at the previous bar and make an intelligent guess.

4

Dolce

mf

5

Steadily

f

Remember—an accidental lasts for a whole bar.

Keep going!

You're doing fine!

You might think that it's cheating to play a piece of sight-reading more than once. But this isn't so, and you can still go on improving your sight-reading even though you have played the piece before. You will find that your sight-reading will improve steadily, so do go back and play all the stages of this book over and over again!

B·E·A·T T·H·E G·R·E·M·L·I·N·S

Musical (or not so musical) gremlins have been at work on this page. They have moved and altered things, so that many of them are now wrong.

Can **you** put everything right?

Draw a ring round anything that is wrong and write the correction underneath.

𝅝 – semibreve

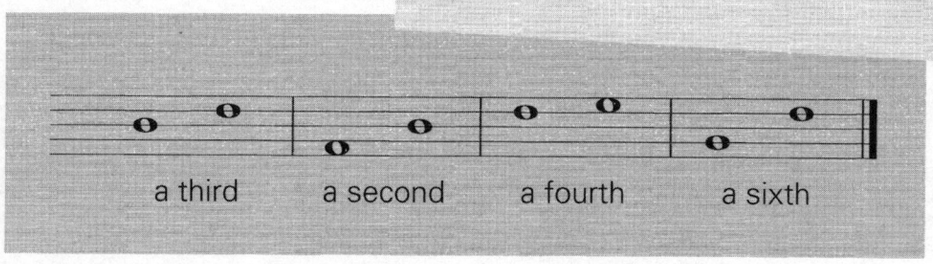

p – loud

f – soft

– getting louder

𝄽 – a two-beat rest

♯ – a sharp sign

♮ – a flat sign

♪ – a quaver

♩ – a crotchet

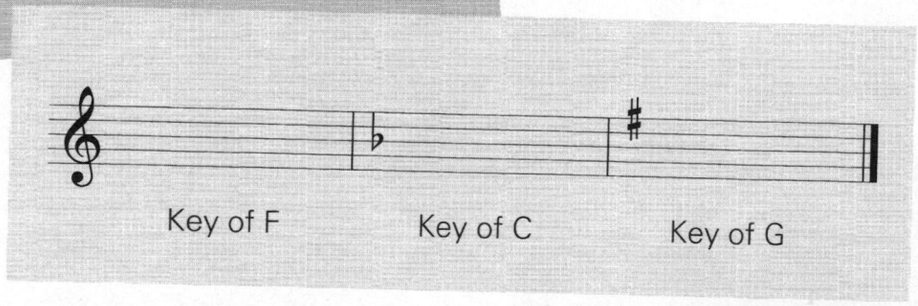

𝅗𝅥 – minim

Printed by
Halstan & Co. Ltd., Amersham, Bucks., England

All the secret code-signs which you have collected on your journey have shown you how to spot and deal with the obstacles that are placed in your way when sight-reading. Don't forget the golden rule—COUNT! GO STEADILY! NEVER LOOK BACK!

CONGRATULATIONS!

You're well on the way to becoming

A Super Sight-reader!

NAME

TEACHER'S SIGNATURE

DATE